SCHIRMER'S LIBRARY OF MUSICAL CLASSICS

Vol. 2146

LUDWIG VAN BEETHOVEN

T0079300

Violin Concerto in D Major, Op. 61

for Violin and Piano Reduction

with online audio of violin & orchestra performances,
and orchestral accompaniments

PLAYBACK+
Speed • Pitch • Balance • Loop

To access audio, visit:
www.halleonard.com/mylibrary

"Enter Code"
1897-9548-9747-0518

performers on the recordings:
Geoffrey Applegate, violin
Stuttgart Symphony
Emil Kahn, conductor

ISBN: 978-1-5400-8891-8

G. SCHIRMER, *Inc.*

DISTRIBUTED BY

Visit Hal Leonard Online at
www.halleonard.com

Contact Us:
Hal Leonard
7777 West Bluemound Road
Milwaukee, WI 53213
Email: info@halleonard.com

In Europe contact:
Hal Leonard Europe Limited
Distribution Centre, Newmarket Road
Bury St Edmunds, Suffolk, IP33 3YB
Email: info@halleonardeurope.com

In Australia contact:
Hal Leonard Australia Pty. Ltd.
4 Lentara Court
Cheltenham, Victoria, 3192 Australia
Email: info@halleonard.com.au

to Stephen von Breuning

Violin Concerto
in D Major, Op. 61

Ludwig van Beethoven
(1770–1827)

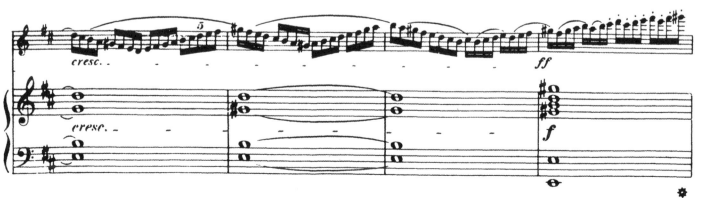

SCHIRMER'S LIBRARY
OF MUSICAL CLASSICS

Vol. 2146

LUDWIG VAN BEETHOVEN

Violin Concerto in D Major, Op. 61

for Violin and Piano Reduction

with online audio of violin & orchestra performances,
and orchestral accompaniments

PLAYBACK+
Speed • Pitch • Balance • Loop

To access audio, visit:
www.halleonard.com/mylibrary

"Enter Code"
6729-7414-1368-0428

performers on the recordings:
Geoffrey Applegate, violin
Stuttgart Symphony
Emil Kahn, conductor

ISBN: 978-1-5400-8891-8

G. SCHIRMER, Inc.

DISTRIBUTED BY

Visit Hal Leonard Online at
www.halleonard.com

Contact Us:
Hal Leonard
7777 West Bluemound Road
Milwaukee, WI 53213
Email: info@halleonard.com

In Europe contact:
Hal Leonard Europe Limited
Distribution Centre, Newmarket Road
Bury St Edmunds, Suffolk, IP33 3YB
Email: info@halleonardeurope.com

In Australia contact:
Hal Leonard Australia Pty. Ltd.
4 Lentara Court
Cheltenham, Victoria, 3192 Australia
Email: info@halleonard.com.au

ABOUT THE CADENZAS

Beethoven wrote no cadenzas for his violin concerto. Dozens of performers and composers for the last two centuries have offered several possibilities. The cadenzas by violinist Fritz Kreisler are among those most often performed and have been included here as a separate inserted part, though any cadenza of choice may be used. To accommodate the many options at cadenza points in the accompaniment recordings, there are a few seconds of silence. This time allows the recording to be paused, a cadenza of choice performed, and then to resume with the orchestra recording.

to Stephen von Breuning

Violin Concerto
in D Major, Op. 61

Ludwig van Beethoven
(1770–1827)

4

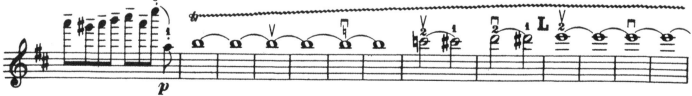

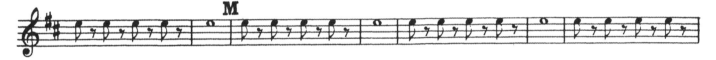

6

* The performance and accompaniment recordings include 10 measures of click as a guide for the soloist.

* On the accompaniment recording, there are a few seconds of silence to allow the player to pause the recording, perform the cadenza of their choice, and resume with the orchestra recording.

* The performance and accompaniment recordings end here.

14

Rondo.

* Two beats of click are given on the accompaniment recording.

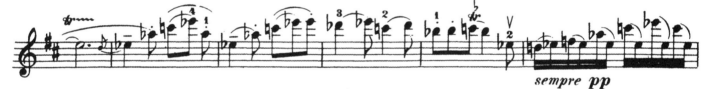

* On the accompaniment recording, there are a few seconds of silence to allow the player to pause the recording, perform the cadenza of their choice, and resume with the orchestra recording.

** Four clicks on the accompaniment recording guide the soloist.

SCHIRMER'S LIBRARY
OF MUSICAL CLASSICS

Vol. 2146

LUDWIG VAN BEETHOVEN

Violin Concerto
in D Major, Op. 61

for Violin and Piano Reduction

with online audio of violin & orchestra performances,
and orchestral accompaniments

performers on the recordings:
Geoffrey Applegate, violin
Stuttgart Symphony
Emil Kahn, conductor

ISBN: 978-1-5400-8891-8

G. SCHIRMER, Inc.

DISTRIBUTED BY

Copyright © 2020 by G. Schirmer, Inc. (ASCAP) New York, NY
International Copyright Secured. All Rights Reserved.

Visit Hal Leonard Online at
www.halleonard.com

Contact Us:
Hal Leonard
7777 West Bluemound Road
Milwaukee, WI 53213
Email: info@halleonard.com

In Europe contact:
Hal Leonard Europe Limited
Distribution Centre, Newmarket Road
Bury St Edmunds, Suffolk, IP33 3YB
Email: info@halleonardeurope.com

In Australia contact:
Hal Leonard Australia Pty. Ltd.
4 Lentara Court
Cheltenham, Victoria, 3192 Australia
Email: info@halleonard.com.au

ABOUT THE CADENZAS

Beethoven wrote no cadenzas for his violin concerto. Dozens of performers and composers for the last two centuries have offered several possibilities. The cadenzas by violinist Fritz Kreisler are among those most often performed and have been included here as a separate inserted part, though any cadenza of choice may be used. To accommodate the many options at cadenza points in the accompaniment recordings, there are a few seconds of silence. This time allows the recording to be paused, a cadenza of choice performed, and then to resume with the orchestra recording.

CADENZAS

I

Fritz Kreisler

Cadenza
Nobilmente

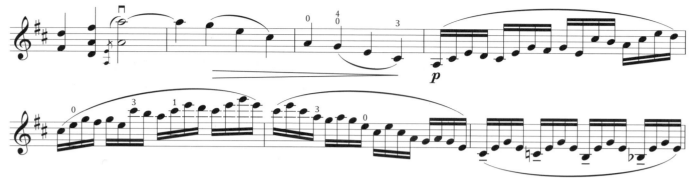

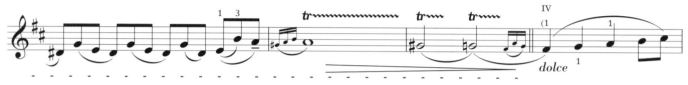

6

II

III

Cadenza

poco a poco cresc.

molto marcato

ff

poco rall. - - - - - -

a tempo

tap   tap   tap   tap Bass.

4 taps (2 measure)
precede music.

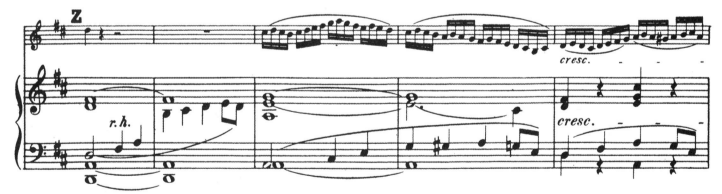

Larghetto.

Attacca subito il Rondo

Rondo.